THE STREET OF CLOCKS

THE STREET OF CLOCKS

Thomas Lux

HOUGHTON MIFFLIN COMPANY
BOSTON NEW YORK 2001

Copyright © 2001 by Thomas Lux

For information about permission to reproduce selections from this book,
write to Permissions, Houghton Mifflin Company, 215 Park Avenue
South, New York, New York 10003.

Visit our Web site: www.houghtonmifflinbooks.com.

Library of Congress Cataloging-in-Publication Data
Lux, Thomas, date.
The street of clocks / Thomas Lux.
p.   cm.
ISBN 0-618-08624-2
I. Title.
PS3562.U87 S77   2001
811'.54 — dc21   00-066976

Printed in the United States of America

WOZ 10 9 8 7 6 5 4 3 2 1

Book design by Melissa Lotfy
Type is FontShop Scala

Many of the poems in this book appeared in the following magazines:
*The Atlantic Monthly, The American Poetry Review, The Kenyon Review,
Shenandoah, Controlled Burn, Poetry International, Washington Square,
Fence, The San Diego Reader, The Harvard Review,* and *The Cider Press
Review.*

*—for Claudia Kilbourne Lux, my daughter,
and for Stephen Dobyns, my friend*

The fact is the sweetest dream that labor knows.

— ROBERT FROST

I am certain of nothing but the holiness of the
Heart's affections and the truth of the Imagination.

— JOHN KEATS

CONTENTS

THE STREET OF CLOCKS

Cucumber Fields Crossed
by High-Tension Wires

The high-tension spires spike the sky
beneath which boys bend
to pick from prickly vines
the deep-sopped fruit, the rind's green
a green sunk
in green. They part the plants' leaves,
reach into the nest,
and pull out mother, father, fat Uncle Phil.
The smaller yellow-green children stay,
for now. The fruit goes
in baskets by the side of the row,
every thirty feet or so. By these bushels
the boys get paid, in cash,
at day's end, this summer
of the last days of the empire
that will become known as
the past, adios, *then*,
the ragged-edged beautiful blink.

The Man into Whose Yard You Should Not Hit Your Ball

each day mowed
and mowed his lawn, his dry quarter-acre,
the machine slicing a wisp
from each blade's tip. Dust storms rose
around the roar, 6 P.M. every day,
spring, summer, fall. If he could mow
the snow he would.
On one side, his neighbors the cows
turned their backs to him
and did what they do to the grass.
Where he worked, I don't know,
but it set his jaw to: tight.
His wife a cipher, shoebox tissue,
a shattered apron. As if
into her head he drove a wedge of shale.
Years later, his daughter goes to jail.
Mow, mow, mow his lawn
gently down a decade's summers.
On his other side lived mine and me,
across a narrow pasture, often fallow—
a field of fly balls, the best part of childhood
and baseball. But if a ball crossed his line,
as one did in 1956
and another in 1958,
it came back coleslaw—his lawnmower
ate it up, happy
to cut something, no matter
what the manual said
about foreign objects,
stones, or sticks.

Plague Victims Catapulted
over Walls into Besieged City

Early germ
warfare. The dead
hurled this way turn like wheels
in the sky. Look: there goes
Larry the Shoemaker, barefoot, over the wall,
and Mary Sausage Stuffer, see how she flies,
and the Hatter twins, both at once, soar
over the parapet, little Tommy's elbow bent
as if in a salute,
and his sister, Mathilde, she follows him,
arms outstretched, through the air,
just as she did on earth.

Bonehead

Bonehead time, bonehead town. Bonehead teachers.
Bonehead mom, bonehead dad, bonehead aunts
and uncles and cousins too.
Bonehead me, bonehead you.
Bonehead books, playground, box lunch, fast food,
tract homes, Sunday school.
Bonehead Truman, McCarthy, Eisenhower too.
Bonehead me, bonehead you.
Bonehead music, TV, H-bomb, movies,
butch cut, tail fins, baby boom.
Bonehead Russia, America, England too.
Bonehead me, bonehead you.

Beauty School

On the Avenue of Fashion
in the noted necropolis, kitty-corner
from a croissant shop
and four blocks down
from a dozen banks,
is the campus of the Beauty School,
where we learn to walk
assuming we are watched
and where, somewhere, in each book
is placed a mirror: *Lost in books,*
we say, late for a study break
date, *I got lost*
in the text. The teacher
stands at the front
of the room: he's the teacher.
The students sit in rows,
those with cheaper haircuts in the rear.
The class is Aesthetics 101.
Beauty is everywhere, the teacher says,
tossing its head.
And when we graduate
the world is there for us, whole, to dread,
to drain.

In the Bedroom Above the Embalming Room

a man sits on the bed's edge in a white T-shirt,
white socks. He is my neighbor,
the local undertaker.
His wife lies behind him, reading a book,
the sheet drawn up above her breasts.
Otherwise, it would be impolite to look.
Or to look I'd wait until they dressed.
From my window they make a kind of X.
I've seen her feed the birds,
but not so much they stay
too long and leave their lime
to stain her deck and waste her time
in washing it away.

So We Can See the Snakes Coming

we cut the lawn
down to the dirt that holds its roots — the aesthetics
of landscape
less important
than the fear for our lives
and our low supplies
of antivenin. Primordial ghost-pulses, so deep
in our cells' root cellars,
so many colliding, lost, and crossing
bloodstreams. . . . Which is why one woman,
so afraid of snakes
she cannot bear to see one, even in pictures,
which is why when
she opened the curtains
of her suburban living room's wide window (with mountain
view), she saw
a dozen snakes loop and lash
atop her flat-top shrubs.
Who was in the herpetarium, her or them?
Some several eons ago, in her family tree,
the tree in which
her family literally lived,
a distant relation
died by snake,
and thereafter one or two each century,
for thousands of centuries,
in this manner also die.
She knows this in her marrow: what she fears
she has reason to fear.

Thomas the Broken-Mouthed

A sack on his back, his burlap shirt flapping in a devil's wind,
Thomas the Broken-Mouthed
walks up and down
the bad land, and amidst the bad believers,
he was born in, and among.
He walks up and down, his big wooden stick striking
the road just ahead of the two still
unsettled puffs of dust
his bare feet raise. Thomas the Broken-Mouthed—called thus
for his lies, say some,
called thus for other reasons, some others say.
In each village two or three fall behind him—disaffected vendors
of drowsy syrups, stiff-fingered cutpurses, sour
camel drivers, well poisoners, and children (milky-skinned,
pockmarked), children of the rich,
of prelates, pushing before them
wooden-wheeled barrows of grain
to bake into bread
to eat on the march. Thomas the Broken-Mouthed has a mission,
within which is a vision,
within which
is a tiny black fire. *Who will pile the drought-dried straw on this fire,*
who will be the naphtha resin,
who will follow the fire,
who will be the sparks with fiery wings for me? asks
Thomas the Broken-Mouthed,
standing on a tree stump that reveals
one hundred rings, one hundred years
that the books now call The Last One Hundred Years.

The Handsome Swamp

knows it's a handsome swamp: the alligators
tell it so, as do the water lilies (always
sycophantic) and their pads. The bug life
stands on its hind legs
and cheers, *Let's live in the handsome swamp!*
The feeders on fish
and the fish food, the oxygen-spewing algae,
the vines, the cypress
and its knees—all are glad.
And the handsome swamp
keeps its handsome up: combing its reeds,
silk-sieving its silt.
The thick black snakes love the handsome swamp.
They speak this to it
as they cruise in grids
on its surface. But now
the green tree frogs,
those of the bright spots on their backs,
sing *no, no, no,* contrarily, all night, *no, no, no.*
This stirs the macaws to clatter; a hornbill
picks a parasite
from beneath his wing
and cracks it with his beak, which sound catches
a big beetle's antennae, and then the monkeys
take up with it (it's always
the *me, me, me* monkeys, greedy
for personification), and, finally, the rats
come out, noses first,
and gather in pods,
sniffing the air.

The Blister Test

They think you're dead but you're not. You're in a coma
or have a rare condition
that mimics death—you feel the pennies,
cool and heavy, on your eyelids,
you sense far-off weeping, but of the three people
here (the town priest, a quack doctor, and somewhat slow
Cousin Freddy) only Freddy *can* weep,
though rarely does so at deaths,
especially deaths in the family. As the doctor rifles
your pockets and the priest, using butter,
pulls a ring from your finger, you wish
Tanta Hedwig were here.
She's sharper than Freddy; she'd insist
(more out of superstition
than in real hope: Dead is dead, Tanta Hedwig
always said) on the blister test: a match
held to the sole
of the deceased's left foot. If it doesn't blister,
you're dead. If it does,
it means you live.
In the case of the former: you go to earth.
In the case of the latter: Mother's family
applies a balm of bark and pith,
which sometimes brings the sleeper back from "the land between."
Father's side
drains the blister
and keeps its fluid in a phial as antidote to dog bite
and complaints of the eye.

From Grade School Window,
Watching Local Bookie Arrested

They led him from his candy store in cuffs, the cops
whose sons played ball with his, for whose teams
his numbers money bought caps and suits.
In *his* suit once, at the cleaner's: two grand,
in a roll, wrapped in rubber bands.
My father and my father's friends bet a buck
or half thereof each day on their lucky digits.
Once, hitting it meant a washing machine,
and dryer, and an orange rug, which made my mother happy,
some. They hauled the bookie out,
to a bigger town nearby—over a mountain,
across a river. He did his time,
ninety days, and when released
(it was his third offense) he never took or made a bet again
until some decades later
in the black black belly of tumors
when the doctor told him: The 8 horse, Quicksand
(out of Leadmine, sired by Tub of Dust),
in the 4th at Aqueduct,
going off at 33 to 1,
bet on him,
bet on that dead horse.

Grain Burning Far Away

The wheat fields blaze, wide waving plains
of them, on fire again, the black burn-line lapping
the gold grain: nature's delete button eating
each letter of each stalk. Over that short mountain
to the north, barley fields ignite,
and to the south, across the salt marshes, acres
and acres of oats
crackle and smoke,
and, it is reported from the east, the long green stands of corn
sawed off at the ankles
by heat. All the flora's, in fact, on fire: onion fields fried
underground, not one turnip unscorched, every root,
bulb, and peanut on the planet boiled
in the soil. Trees burn
like matches, but faster, orchids die
when the fire's still a mile away. Seaweed, too,
and the kelp beds
from the top down blacken like candle wicks; spinach, in cans,
when opened, is ash. Moss melts,
hedgerows explode, every
green thing on earth
on fire and still all smoke jumpers snug,
asleep, undisturbed, the fire station's pole cold,
palmless, the fire extinguisher fat
with foam. Hear it snap,
the red angry fire,
hear it take the air and turn it into pain,
see the flame's blue, bruised heart
never waver, waver, never waver.

The Doldrum Fracture Zone

The place where sailors — though now open
to all professions — went to consider the mirage
of their own despair. Once, only sailors *could*
go there: the breezeless place,
the weed-choked and stinking sea plain
where they stalled for weeks, months. Today,
the Zone comes to us,
its great gray inertness dragged
like opaque knife wounds over each
who stands on a shore and calls it in,
dragged over him or her who believes his or her despair *is*
a mirage and not
a mirror. . . . That man
who still holds the handle of the mailbox open, its huge black mouth
having just swallowed
a letter that cannot be unwritten
which falls on top of a pile of other such letters
in their white dresses
in the dark — that man has called it in.
There is a sound of tiny roots being torn,
and a water spider, skating smoothly over the Zone's flat surface, sinks.

The Nerve Doctors

Here they come by the busload, the nerve doctors.
Some journey overland
(many die on mountain passes),
some take the river routes, some fly
(after dosing on Veronal),
some just send their brains
or disciples, a few walk all night
across salt plains. They continue
to arrive — every hotel room
two to a bed in nerve doctors,
three deep at the bar of every saloon,
and still they disembark
for the convention,
their big meeting. It's election year
and all the nerve doctors are here — there's a group
from China, and that huddle
over there, they came by train
from Omaha, Nebraska, USA.
The three from France seem to be in psychic pain.
The nerve doctors stand in small aggregations,
nodding, rocking on the balls
of their feet, consulting (each one says
when another finishes a sentence, *I have listened*) about
the election, and about who
the next nerve doctors' president will be,
and where — since it is his choice — the next
nerve doctors' convention
shall be held.

The Poison Shirt

You put it on to walk the bright day, dumb
to the little skull-
and-crossbones
buttons, dumb to pulmonary numbing, half-hazy eye, rubber
ankles, not
noticing the sound
of people slumping—*shhump*—to the sidewalk
three seconds
after you pass. Each moment slimmer than nil—so the day passes, too,
with its trail of the poisoned
that ends with the you
in the poison shirt.

The Road That Runs Beside the River

follows the river as it bends
along the valley floor,
going the way it must.
Where water goes, so goes the road,
if there's room (not in a ravine,
gorge), the river
on your right or left. Left is better: when you're driving,
it's over your elbow across
the road.
You see the current, which is
what the river *is:* the river
in the river, a thing sliding fast forward
inside a thing sliding not so fast forward.
Driving with, beside, the river's flow is good.
Another pleasure, driving against it: it's the same river
someone else will see
somewhere else downstream — same play,
new theater, different set.
Wide, shallow, fairly fast,
roundy-stone streambed, rocky-land river,
it turns there or here — the ground
telling it so — draining dull
mountains to the north,
migrating, feeding a few hard-fleshed fish
who live in it. One small sandbar splits
the river, then it loops left,
the road right, and the river's silver
slips under the trees,
into the forest,
and over the sharp perpendicular
edge of the earth.

A Kiss

One wave, falling forward, meets another wave falling
forward. Well water,
hand-hauled, mineral, cool, could be
a kiss, or pastures
fiery green after rain, before
the grazers. The kiss—like a shoal of fish whipped
one way, another way, like the fever dreams
of a million monkeys—let the kiss
carry me, closer than your carotid artery, to you.

A Bird, Whose Wingtips Were on Fire,

led the small boy, lost in the forest at night,
to the clearing's edge
where the search teams
were gathering to look for him.
He ran to his weeping mother and father,
who raised him in their arms,
and all gathered around in great joy—the neighbors,
the cops, soldiers,
sailors, field hands, blood-
hounds, the high school marching band, all
circled the boy in great joy until
he talked of the bird
that came to him as he sat shivering
beside a moss-graced boulder,
second night lost
in the woods. No one wanted to hear that,
even in their relief
no one wanted to believe
a bird with flaming wingtips
lit a path
and led the boy on it to safety. Better
that it was dumb luck or, as many murmur,
the will of a being
with a short one-syllable name.
What color was the bird? Did it speak to you?,
they asked the boy. Gray-brown, said the boy,
and no, it didn't speak, birds
don't talk. Were you playing with matches,
and did you set a bird on fire
which then flew away,

and you followed?, they asked the boy.
No matches, no hunger,
the boy said, and the only things that scared me
were the orchids and a fawn.

Shotgun Loaded with Rock Salt

So I took my shotgun
loaded with rock salt, to sting and burn
but not likely kill
the boys who rob my vines, my two peach trees
that survived the drought
and this year set their first fruit, about a bushel is all,
still hard as golf balls.
Your cuke vines was growing on our side of the fence,
that big boy said last time.
Yeah, and my mushmelons just rolled over your side too? I said.
He said, Nope, *they* bounced.
I never did like his father either when we were coming up. Once
I pulled him, half drowned, from the river.
Paper said I saved his life.
He didn't say a damn thing.
I thought about that
as I sent a double barrelful of salt
to say goodbye
to my peaches
and that big boy's fat ass.

Slimehead (*Hoplostethus atlanticus*)

Humans eat first with their ears, so
to sell this deep-sea fish
we give some poetry to its name: orange roughy.
Oh tasty, despite its mucus-exuding head—that's gone
long before your dinner plate. A mild meat,
firm, low fat,
fished a mile beneath the waves.
Slow-growing, long-lived: up to 150 years.
In the lightless depths
it's brown, not orange. When you pull it up
each blood vessel bursts,
in its version of the bends?
I ate it, twice.
I'll eat it again
when it's over being overfished, if so.
But rather than its flanks
sautéed in this or that,
I'd like to roll inside a shoal
of them, down there where nobody goes,
to know what they know,
to not know what I know,
down there with the hoki, hake,
rattail, oreo dory, my dear slimeheads
and their countrymen,
the shy, prolific squid.

Pre-Cerebral

(— C. W.)

No ideas. No thoughts, nor
philosophy. Hunger, thirst,
yes, flight and fear. And sound, touch,
and sight, and the tongue, which tastes.
Ten fingers, the heart's in place.
Two arms, legs, esophagus.
Looking down: that's the sweet swale.
Looking up: that's the wide sky.
Mile after mile, the wide sky.
And touch. And the tongue, which tastes.

Salve

Paint me with it,
he tells the nurse,
and calls, too, for balm,
ointment, slather it all
(and add some tincture) on him.
In the soft moth powder of it
swathe him, swathe him, on white sheets,
in a white room. Some unguent
on his clavicle, please, nurse,
and on each ventricle lotion would be good.
To each temple: assuagement.
To the bony corners of his eye sockets, your fingers,
nurse, to press there anodynes.
Pour a river (with rivulets)
of emollients from his nape
down his spine's valley—let a pool
fill there, a shallow pond
of salve, let it gather there,
then place a tiny boat
upon its eastern shore, nurse,
and launch it westward, gently, with your thumb.

Jungleside

Beside the jungle he builds a house of cinderblock,
brick, steel, and stone — to keep the jungle out,
which he lives beside, *in*side
a clearing cut from its heart, its green sweat and soup.
A colony of creepers poke their noses
to his window, a vine strangles
the chimney — to close its throat
and smoke him out. He chops
a tree's arms off, peels
back the fronds and ferns that press huge hands
against his door. A tendril,
tentative, probes like a hunting snake,
like a fingertip, a tongue, through his keyhole.
Ripe threads ooze between cracks a breeze could not. . . .
First he burned it, the jungle, slashed it back,
carved from it his acre
and built a house.
To insult it, he planted beans in rows.
To insult it, he seeded then mowed his lawn.
He wanted the jungle to want its jungle back.
He wanted to lean his hard shoulder
against its hard shoulder.
What happened? After the ants
cleaned his skull of flesh,
a sapling grew through its left eye socket
and, as it strained for light, it lifted
his skull up, head-high, a tilt (you can see
it there, it will talk) to it, a deferential nod
to the jungle, unovercome.

Regarding (Most) Songs

> Whatever is too stupid to say
> can be sung.
> —JOSEPH ADDISON (1672–1719)

The human voice can sing a vowel to break your heart.
It trills a string of banal words,
but your blood jumps, regardless. You don't care
about the words but only *how* they're sung
and the music behind—the brass, the drums.
Oh the primal, necessary drums
behind the words so dumb!
That power, the bang and the boom and again the bang
we cannot, need not, live without,
nor without other means to make sweet noise,
the guitar or violin, the things that sing
the plaintive, joyful sounds.
Which is why I like songs best
when I can't hear the words, or, better still,
when there are no words at all.

A Voiceless Parrot Learns to Read
and Write and Play the Trumpet

He can't learn to speak—to make the sounds that mimic
words—which causes the man
who gives him seeds
to no longer give him seeds
and to leave ajar his cage door. The years
that follow tell the story: no matter what, each day
he goes to the library, where he teaches himself first the alphabet,
then words,
then sentences, and then
to write. He reads and reads
and writes and writes (eating book glue
and the husks of nuts
the pigeons leave behind) alone in the stacks
until the day he hears a noise
so high and true
his flight feathers tense. It's the King coming,
and the sound the sound
of those who herald him with horns of brass.
He loves, instantly, that noise.
How is he going to finger-work the valves?
How does he turn his beak into lips?
About the size of small plums,
how can his little parrot lungs
fill and exhale and make
the sound that floods
the marrow bones and blood
(every cell, each platelet) with such high
and piercing light?

Beggar's Bowl Stolen

Gone with it: one thin coin (400
buy a litchi nut), a hairpin.
The three flies, sentinels
on its rim — they're gone too.
A small blue bowl, scratched,
dull. The beggar's still here.
The beggar's still here but blind
and didn't see who stole his bowl.

A Man Gets Off Work Early

and decides to snorkel in a cool mountain lake.
Not as much to see
as in the ocean, but it's tranquil (no sharks) floating
face down into that other world.
The pines' serrated shadows reach
across the waters,
and just now, just below him, to his left,
a pickerel, long and sharp and . . . *whuppa whuppa whuppa*, loud,
louder, behind him, above him, the water, louder,
whuppa whuppa whuppa. . . . Two weeks later,
twenty miles away, he's found,
a cinder, his wetsuit
melted on him, in a crablike position
on the still warm ash
of the forest floor
through which fire tore unchecked,
despite the chemicals,
the men with axes and shovels,
despite the huge scoops of lake water
dropped on it
from his friend the sky,
on whom he turned his back.

Baby, Still Crying, Swallowed by a Snake

Big snake, medium-sized baby,
head first, face up
between snake's unhinged jaws — its sharp-spined
conveyor belt calling baby down
to its belly's burning acid bath.
Bye-bye, baby,
oh Lord, baby, bye-bye.

Rommel's Asparagus

(Normandy, 1945)

The glidermen died, their gliders were riven
when they dropped
from the sky, at night,
into the clearings,
which were not clear
but studded with posts: Rommel's Asparagus,
which tore the wings off
or crushed the nose of
or cleaved the cabin of
(the soldiers inside from throat to toe torn)
the gliders
as they slid from the sky
(hoping to skid on their bellies to a stop)
behind enemy lines,
the same enemy who built these spikes, spines,
on his back
so he could turn his full face to the sea.

Plastic Castle in Goldfish Bowl

Inside, the princess is prisoner
in her second-floor suite. Not
of her father, the king, downstairs
asleep on his throne (little bubbles rising
from his mouth), not
of the knife-and-bone prince
she refuses to marry, nor
of vague neurasthenic complaints
or a face pickaxed by smallpox. No,
she is prisoner
of the goldfish,
which is a big fish: she's a tidbit
to him. The moat's
drowned, the drawbridge up and drowned. The god
who drops the fish food flakes,
those gifts from above
the water, is gone. The goldfish
wants to kiss the princess, his lips
say so, and his big,
glutinous, glassy eye at her window,
being lidless, never blinks.

Stubblefield Dusted with Snow

The corn is cut, chopped—leaf, stalk, and cob—then sent
as sweet silage
to the silos,
and now, late February, hard
as the hammered head of a spike, the ground
is brown and holds against it
the lighter brown
of the punji-pointed stubs. This is the season
of doubt. Add a dusting of snow, light-
as-sea-foam snow. And a little wind,
cold. Add the low
sound said wind makes, sometimes, along the rows, and add
the snow's skirt slightly lifted,
then let down, sighing.
This is the season of doubt. Add, also, a human
this, a human that.

The Downslope Winds

The Congo, the Amazon, the Mississippi—big
rivers!—of winds crest
high peaks and then avalanche down
the downslopes, sped
by gravity and battering
the foothills and flatlands below: chinook, zonda,
foehn, Santa Ana, simoom, *xlokk*, sirocco,
brickfielder, khamsin—embolism winds,
winds of rage, suicide, migraines,
madness (a viable defense
for murder, Wyoming, 1850s), often hot, always
dry, the thin-lipped poisoner winds
that roll down on us, buzz
our breastbones, roll
over us: the lacerate,
the enfilading
winds.

A Library of Skulls

Shelves and stacks and shelves of skulls, a Dewey
decimal number inked on each unfurrowed forehead.
Here's a skull
who, before he lost his fleshy parts
and lower bones, once
walked beside a river (we're in the poetry section
now), his head full of love
and loneliness; and this smaller skull,
in the sociology stacks, smiling (they're all
smiling) — it's been empty
a hundred years. That slot
across another's temple? An ax blow
that fractured
her here. Look at this one from the children's shelves,
a baby, his fontanel
a screaming mouth and this time no teeth, no smile.
Here are a few (history): a murderer,
and this one — see how close their eye sockets! — a thief,
and here's a rack of torturers' skulls
beneath which a longer, much longer, row of the tortured.
And look: generals' row,
their epaulets
on the shelves to each side of them.
Shelves and shelves, stacks stacked on top of stacks,
floor above floor,
this towering high-rise library
of skulls, not another bone in the place,
and just now the squeak of a wheel
on a cart piled high with skulls
on their way back to shelves,

while in the next aisle
a cart is filling with those about to be loaned
to the tall, broken-hearted man waiting
at the desk, his library card
face down before him.

Marine Snow at Mid-Depths and Down

As you descend, slowly, falling faster past
you, this snow,
ghostly, some flakes bio-
luminescent (you plunge,
and this lit snow doesn't land
at your feet but keeps falling below
you): single-cell-plant chains, shreds
of zooplankton's mucus foodtraps, dust motes,
fishy fecal pellets, radioactive fallout, soot,
sand grains, pollen. . . . And inside
these jagged falling islands
live more micro-lives,
which feed creatures
on the way down
and all the way down. And you,
in your sinking isolation
booth, you go down, too,
through this food-snow, these shards, blown-off
bits of planet, its flora
and flesh, you
slip straight down, unreeled,
until the bottom's oozy silt, the sucking
baby-soft muck,
welcomes you
to the deep sea's bed,
a million anvils per square inch
pressing on your skull.
How silent here, how much life,
few places deeper on earth,
none with more width.

An Erg

Face down, face down,
in an erg, the dead punished middle
of the Great Samboosa Erg, gone.
A sand flea in a sea of sand
is still a sand flea, and sand
is what flies in the wind,
needles to your skin,
and when the wind falls
the sand falls, too.
What is dust, lighter, hovers
in the air's slightest trembles.
Stones don't move, much. Boulders
never do. It all—dust, sand,
stones—comes from the mountains.
Worn from, carved from, torn from.
Where do things go when they die here,
and what eats them when they do?
Nowhere. Many things. The sun.
No shortage of bones
and the sandblasted corpses
of cars, trucks. . . . At night,
cold as an ice pick's tip,
under a dome of black
so large even Allah could not dream it,
marches a line of scorpions,
many miles long, single file
over the dunes, the curlicues
of each tail lighted
by poison's little lamp.

The War of Jenkins's Ear

(1739–1741)

Captain Jenkins lost his ear—that is,
had it severed, by cutlass,
a Spanish seaman's. It flopped
like a shot bird next to Jenkins's foot.
He carried it in a velvet box
to the House of Commons
and with it started a war
that had nothing to do
with commerce, trading rights,
boundary disputes, profits.
A war fought over an insult to an ear,
what one man can do to another man,
and what he cannot, nothing more, no, nothing
more. On the flag that led his outraged men
to battle: an ear, pink
on blue background. It flapped
in the wind of musket fire,
it urged men onward,
Remember Jenkins's ear, boys, remember
Jenkins's ear!

Lucky

One sweet pound of filet mignon
sizzles on the roadside. Let's say a hundred yards below
the buzzard. The buzzard
sees no cars or other buzzards
between the mountain range due north
and the horizon to the south,
and across the desert west and east
no other creature's nose leads it to this feast.
The buzzard's eyes are built for this: he can see the filet is raw
and he likes the sprig
of parsley in this brown and dusty place.
No abdomens to open here before he eats.
No tearing, slashing with his beak,
no offal-wading
to pick and rip the softest parts.
He does not need to threaten or screech
to keep the other buzzards from his meat.
He circles slowly down,
not a flap, not a shiver in his wide wings,
and lands before his dinner, an especially lucky buzzard,
who bends his neck to pray, then eats.

The Fish-Strewn Fields

After the river rose above its banks, after the farms
and fields and yards
were drowned and drained again, all
was fish-strewn, stump- and root-strewn,
besotted. Here and there,
pieces of an upriver town—light blue ice tray,
birdhouse, the town clerk—all litter the pastures.
Aerial photos (only mud now, no water for boats,
no ground to walk on) show
us this, the helicopter dropping close
to look for anything alive.
The town clerk's blue shirt blooms.
He drank deep of the waters and mud.
The river recedes now, back between,
then below its banks,
and recedes still more, drains to the stones,
then through the bedrock beneath its sand, oh, it sinks,
the river, it's gone,
and then the banks close like the lips of a wound,
leaving a wormy scar
along the bottom of our valley
for miles, miles.

Shoreless

No pier, peninsula, nor mainland near.
A cargo of parrots
squawk in the hold
and, topside, bananas rot. What we convey
we'll soon need to eat.
The compass cries we're drifting west
where we know land lies,
and the distance the stars said we've made
puts us inland a hundred miles.
Something's broken—the compass? The stars?
We're not on land, unless the waves are wheat,
unless they're gold, not green.
Is that the sextant in the slop bucket?
The wind's high but the sails slack.
The first parrot's plucked.
His little pile of party feathers blows across the deck.
Who's that sack of bones perched on a pegleg?
Who's that craning from the crow's nest?

Unlike, for Example, the Sound
of a Riptooth Saw

gnawing through a shinbone, a high howl
inside of which a bloody, slashed-by-growls note
is heard, unlike *that*
sound, and instead, its opposite: a barely sounded
sound (put your nuclear ears
on for it, your giant hearing horn, its cornucopia mouth
wide) — a slippery whoosh of rain
sliding down a mirror
leaned against a windfallen tree stump, the sound
a child's head makes
falling against his mother's breast,
or the sound, from a mile away, as the town undertaker
lets Grammy's wrist
slip from his grip
and fall to the shiny table. And, if you turn
your head just right
and open all your ears,
you might hear
this *finest* sound, this lost sound: a plow's silvery prow
cleaving the earth (your finger
dragging through milk, a razor
cutting silk) like a clipper ship cuts the sea.
If you do hear this sound,
then follow it with your ear and also your eye
as it and the tractor that pulls it
disappear over a hill
until it is no sound at all,
until it comes back over the hill again,
again dragging its furrow,
its ground-rhythm, its wide open throat, behind it.

Cordon Sanitaire

The blanch place, pale, like under a bandage,
a creamy strip of peace
quarantined between cannons like bristles,
like combs' teeth
aligned across from each other. *It's balmy here
in Cordon Sanitaire,* the general wrote
on a postcard, sitting on the veranda
of the Cordon Sanitaire Hotel and Spa. *All's neutral,
a very light, wind-worn tan
the one color.* The back door
of a cannon, the one that swings open
so that a man can insert
a large large shell — Did I,
he thought, did I just hear one
open? *I ate the veal
last night, mashed potatoes, some florets
of cauliflower.* He didn't mention,
or else an editor struck it from the text,
the black smoke
flowing from the high stacks on low buildings;
he didn't mention
the little song he sang: "Leprosaria, Crematoria,
Adiosia, in Memoria."
His secretary, who was there,
his last unmarried daughter, there also,
said he didn't actually sing
but made its rhythms seem "liturgical."
He'd even "bounce a little" in his chair,
his daughter said,
until the sky turned to lead, she said, until
the sky turned to lead.

Henry Clay's Mouth

Senator, statesman, Speaker of the House,
exceptional dancer, slim,
graceful, ugly. Proclaimed, before most, slavery
an evil, broker
of elections (burned Jackson
for Adams), took a pistol ball in the thigh
in a duel, delayed by forty years,
with his compromises, the Civil War,
gambler ("I have always
paid peculiar homage to the fickle goddess"),
booze hound, ladies' man—which leads us
to his mouth, which was huge,
a long slash across his face
with which he ate and prodigiously drank,
with which he modulated his melodic voice,
with which he liked to kiss and kiss and kiss.
He said: "Kissing is like the presidency,
it is not to be sought and not to be *declined*."
A rival, one who wanted to kiss
whom he was kissing, said: "The ample
dimensions of his kissing apparatus
enabled him to *rest* one side of it
while the other was on active duty."
If women had the vote,
it was written, if women had the vote,
he would have been President,
kissing everyone in sight,
dancing on tables ("a grand Terpsichorean
performance . . ."), kissing everyone,
sometimes two at once, kissing everyone,
the almost President
of our people.

The Language Animal

Because he can speak, because he can use his words, a whole headful
of them, he gives everything
names, even things that call themselves,
forever, something else.
Because he can speak he can efficiently lie,
or obscure with such brilliance
a listener with less language
is glad to lose more of it.
Because he can speak
he will be lonely
because those who speak back speak another language
of other derivations.
Because he can speak he speaks.
Because he can speak he can pray out loud.
Because he can speak the predators are drawn to him in the night.
Because he can speak
he invented the ear, then two, to better hear himself speak.
Because he can speak he thought he could sing.
Because he can speak
he has one more thing to do
besides searching for food,
or hiding so as not to *be* food.
Because he can speak he draws a full breath
and speaks,
in sentences, each one beginning with a large letter
and ending with a period,
or the soon-to-be-invented marks
that indicate bewilderment and awe.

Pencil Box Shaped Like a Gun

You brought to school that fall
the pistol-shaped pencil box, .45-
caliber-inspired but larger, swollen, loaded
with pens, six-inch ruler, the compass tool—the one
with which you got to stab the paper
and make the stubby pencil
strapped to its other leg move around in a perfect circle.
Also an eraser,
like the rubber hammer
the doctor plunked your knee with
once or twice a year. Blue, a see-through
plastic pencil box atop
the scarred (your uncle Larry's name dug deep) desk,
strata after strata of shellac. . . . The classroom's large
light-filled windows bright,
and Linda Miller's voice
rasps over a speaker, a box with dials, connected
by wire to where she lives,
two or three miles away, over a small river,
halfway up the long grade
of some stubby, stony hills.
Linda's ill, very ill.
We strain to hear
her voice. The teacher talks to the box,
to Linda, whom we hear brokenly
this autumn
of bright skies,
of hay stacked to the rafters,
of swollen pumpkins and gourds,
and of the last cabbages

waiting, any day now,
stripped of their outer leaves,
to become part of
a tasty soup.

The Corner of Paris and Porter

Meet me there, you remember, the corner
of Paris and Porter. We stood on that spot
after walking our city all day,
dropped-off-the-earth lost each in the other.
We'd live in the house there, we said,
we loved the sway-back porch, the elms
in the yard towering. We stopped
in the thick, still shade of one,
the sidewalk raised and cracked by its roots.
On the curb: a mailbox, agape, flag up,
a dry birdbath in the yard,
and in the driveway a yellow car: this was lucky,
a yellow car, a child once told me.
The sunlight a wall slamming down
outside the shade's circle. Two old sisters, we guessed,
lived there: two
lace antimacassars
on two wicker porch chairs.
We'd knock on the door,
tell them we love their house,
which they'd then bequeath to us,
on the corner, the house
we found by chance, chirps and childcalls,
the clanking of lunch dishes,
though we saw not one child or bird.
The mailman (we never saw him but knew his name
was Steve) would leave great piles
of letters, the grocery
and the garden would provide.
It was the corner
of Paris and Porter,

in that part of the city
where we'd never walked before—it was south
and farther south, past downtown,
beyond the meat district, the fish market,
past the street of clocks, the tripe stalls,
the brick kilns, the casket factories; we turned
east, a few blocks north,
there was nothing but warehouses
and long blocks of lots,
tall fences topped by barbed wire, behind which
what? We walked over a bridge
(the train tracks beneath were thick with weeds)
and there it was: a neighborhood—houses,
yards, shrubs, we were talking and talking,
I don't know how many miles, lost
in each the other,
and though we did not know where we were,
we knew where we were going: the corner
of Paris and Porter, remember, the day was blue
and clear, I recall the exact path of an ant,
the mica glinting in the curbstone, a curtain
parting momentarily at your laugh.
I could have drowned in your hair.
Meet me there,
today, don't be late, on the corner
of Paris and Porter.

The Bandage Factory

Our bandage factory's busy: boxcar after boxcar
of gauze-only trains
empty at the east side unloading dock.
The women wash and fold and sterilize.
The men make the big looms boom
in the bandage room.
And the boys and girls (when we're busy
no one goes to school) stack
and sweep and gather scraps
that we ship downstate
to the babies' and children's bandage works.
On the west side loading dock
at five o'clock,
when we've filled a whole train,
we like to stand there
while it pulls away
(some of the children wave)
and watch our bandages go
out into the world
where the wounds reside,
which they were made to dress.

NOTES

The words of the title "Grain Burning Far Away" were put in that order by Robert Steiner.

"The Downslope Winds" owes a debt to Jan DeBlieu's book *Wind*.

The second line of "Shoreless" is borrowed from my friend Robert Winner.

"Henry Clay's Mouth" owes a debt to Paul Johnson's *A History of the American People*.